to be hung from the ceiling

by strings of varying length

to be hung from the ceiling by strings of varying length

rick reid

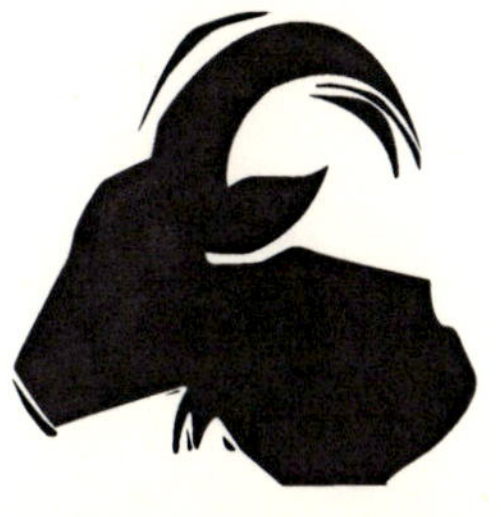

Black Goat
Los Angeles

BLACK GOAT is an independent poetry imprint of Akashic Books created and curated by award-winning Nigerian author Chris Abani. Black Goat is committed to publishing well-crafted poetry and will focus on experimental and thematically challenging work. The series aims to create a proportional representation of female and non-American poets, with an emphasis on Africans. Series titles include:

Abstraktion und Einfühlung by Percival Everett
Auto Mechanic's Daughter by Karen Harryman
Conduit by Khadijah Queen
Controlled Decay by Gabriela Jauregui
eel on reef by Uche Nduka
Gomer's Song by Kwame Dawes

This is a work of fiction. All names, characters, places, and incidents are a product of the author's imagination. Any resemblance to real events or persons, living or dead, is entirely coincidental.

Published by Akashic Books

ISBN-13: 978-1-933354-76-7
Library of Congress Control Number: 2008937357

First printing

Black Goat
c/o Akashic Books
PO Box 1456
New York, NY 10009
info@akashicbooks.com
www.akashicbooks.com

○

•

as seen a wave is not
the same as a wave nor
a day as
temperature

a day as seen
living far

•

o

•

not seen
staring sky
light ' between
circling hour

serial as machine
a living

•

○

•

the accent done
light cut
of a room begun
at distance

here
being storms
over blue and pace
actual caught
climate ' metallic

imprints of raindrop

stolen until time

having then
thin sure

•

o

•

shard
holding ' after glare
in angling away

for example the piano

unweave of cold
thought while
notes a

turning of gaps

someone wrote in curve
as corner as
sculpture
as object

a rain even view like
chalk straying anchor—

slant

itself told
steal of

flammable time

unknowingly open
a view

•

○

•

sketch of telling
whole pieces
advance / shudder

to walls and under

of color
of moment
silence
of minute
as you

have and abandoning
numbers

asleep

a red chair

plain from water
line   upwards

through stoppage and
collecting
to hear reflection

•

o

•

seven and vacant
hours over back breezed
hearing *q*

clatter of the air

---

the unnoticed black
everywhere

•

o

•

fast at darkness
being so

caused—or—beauty

trained through
to turn around
a fixed space
of once
or there

•

o

•

and tangle
knowing these

stream of traffic
as passing still

a place never been

•

○

•

at me the things made
hesitate

•

o

•

it can be
seized be run
away

words of
material is past

is lost ' is

•

o

•

fluent with the less
air   weave
bound

as beginning
begun

•

○

•

dried and blown
crab or sun
drunk or drear
at a place

regardless and
being ‘ hears so

a woman
standing   shore

•

○

•

of hiss or
quiet a letter
or air apart
again

crossed in
by a path
a drove

•

o

•

as a step squares
a sure gray

of ground pressed into
the picture so

not seen is
seeing

•

°

•

a voice carried
through the door
unstaged

birds brass
doorknob before
‘ towed

by wind

•

o

•

the shadow
nature of yet '

a certain thing

willingness to dance
blue usual

a space
about a trapdoor

a listen sleep on the rest
of a couch

the back of a book

•

o

•

a picture

accurate and

cold
at hand

paused

landscape of
again—begin

a stop desire

between
leaves or green

time of
year window for the black

shape of inhabits

•

○

•

the song not
played playing
the known
announcement of not

known blue
yard of crickets
would be

trees seeing

through the door
twice at once

a sky lined
before
or notes of
once now

•

○

•

they are on the day
asleep a
conversation

white — run — walls

twice wheres of
cold the memory was

•

○

•

the not time seen in others
though time
here there

•

o

•

past tends
in case of
glass fire *say*

breaking deep

having been yet
being here

october as scarlet

a hand raised
myself of

a shore of tile
sprayed dream of dots
only appear

‘ time lived

a clock in
the wall first a man

across a second hand

river

•

o

•

the water disks
sent oil
in oil

•

o

•

not means of
time led
by having

missed skin
yesterday ' sun rain

the measure of not
worn clothes

the painted over
fence ' advanced

in sway going train

score wadding up
the tapped out
solo made living

•

o

•

or left
in the rafters ‘ dew

an insert storm

left
burning

•

o

•

swung us flags
the pole top

of stair turns

another stair

well away on home
passing

on   time

•

○

•

step blue
over

cry from the bridge
left its word
behind second

air they
turned as
where it went

•

○

•

in time
known
more

less   end
greens invisible or
first

attention

•

o

•

lie one wave
remember
the shore ' sky

•

○

•

not this in fingers

•

o

•

the wheel by
glass
a river

leaving left

arrives

•

o

•

square a square

shot or sung
with light

•

o

•

a drop
stayed ground staying
weather

a day number envelope
under door

scratch white

the change
home ' met place

patterned radio
leaving and leaving
the station to

be seen looking

•

o

•

out a window turned
away ‘ stops

seeing through
being colored such film

again reflection

dining room
to dining

room a few
more winters

•

○

•

came out
a room
still speaking

could say part
of the body say
overlooking

from a rail

a dress buried
by water buried

wind written *you*
on a line assuming

one
just assume

•

o

•

rain dust
only
beams

high from
the left day

rings moved
in side
of hour

facing profile

•

o

•

further that
they're there

are their
time is

than here
they're out

•

○

•

snow with
axe woods

body with match
shore with

sheet after
sheet kneeling

upon water

•

o

•

relates
in minute by
point done

with too across

shade become
where jays

down the hands
the while

•

o

•

also veering
mark next alley
doors ‘ way

the marsh refers
its sun itself

•

o

•

the days
tear

from their
pages daily from

calendars

•

o

•

the bridge now
in voice

long underwater

•

o

•

aging ages
here in ‘ bodies new
read

change there
exchange days

to resolve
divide   stay

•

o

•

forwarding
a den
played time is maybe

hemmed—crossed

of home having never
seen the day

turn myself

in night the
closing open

reach or stood
dual

•

o

•

broke morning
cannot blue

the bulb burned

where the bee
sleeps
light tilts
from ear

•

o

•

to june in
the whole day *redden*

•

o

•

played instruments in
the would color
from *letter* or

glass wax
from wood

•

°

•

a less night dark is dawn

•

o

•

a passenger sun
left with this

lettered sleep

•

°

•

a ray
glance the block
light

your floor

after ' one

•

o

•

first shadow
thinks ‘ before
city

the half light day

opposing now

and now

•

o

•

a once song at

once

•

o

•

a glass happens

the window
line blue

while once
the city

runs when
returning

•

○

•

a mark left
in water by
water

rill of skin

•

o

•

face of nine
silent—*malic*

the sheer as alive
in the wall ' eye

wells uncertain

a part

•

o

•

feet drawn in the cold

•

o

•

stole of air
approached speaking
a laugh

then through

vent ' behind gates by
gaslight

•

○

•

another owl
wasps home

only appears doesn't
decide

•

o

•

edge of waying figures itself bowing

•

o

•

rocks thrown
—back ‘ toward
memory raining

rooms fogged
in twelve

glass insects

•

o

•

dance cannon
or dear slowly

carrying ‘ nearing
plans a line *here*

drawing the exacting
done the wish
in thicket arms

boxes answering
an orange-black before
waking rust

a way to
the taller yet

speaking halls
lines and far time
tearing dyes

‘ waits

•

o

•

makes eel the
spins ‘ whole makes
blades the green
then

news   may

•

o

•

sign the wall
without name

send the letter
of the spill

—ed can

•

o

•

shape of the bird in
the vein ‘ nick

the wheel shared as diving
of lawn   day
of the hands

flooded once

into body
‘ bloomed

•

o

•

fall

—[illegible] gravity of paper

•

o

•

cigarette shops ash kiss and the sun sun and the sun shut down close'

•

o

•

‘ significance of having not dreamt of not having dreamt of hammering

•

○

•

push door of
' sound

the mind can't draw
up fingers

•

o

•

the dirt stopped
in the page ‘ face
by the sun by
eye by the cover

there the bird drawn

•

o

•

they are working now

wind ‘ not wind

•

o

•

blue over den

spiders come with
warmth

castles upside ‘ own
∂rawn

•

o

•

the deer from the yard

laughter

•

o

•

remain ‘

loosed

•

o

•

the mill of bodies
ends here ‘

in the iron
runs

the smoke of a face

i-n-g

•

o

•

excess shaked

from pigs

the flowers
in passed

•

°

•

sang in the door

today here I lie for tomorrow I'll be
in heaven

trampling

•

o

•

lost on the lip

—of shelf lured

or bonfire

•

o

•

a body of water
in stone

a corridor
night

•

o

•

pour the glass
out the glass so

your hands until
red ‘ stayed in

•

o

•

could see night only
after day

tongu'd-less

•

o

•

no drawing
call it

nite

•

○

•

night *also* sun

•

o

•

the difficult

a fever try

kind coming
up the drive

a portrait of

such colds

•

o

•

went down the hill

went sung
in suitcoat wearing

at all

•

o

•

for the till mid / after
noon a rain

—ed table ‘ scroll

tending the parts

•

o

•

cache ‘ cloud ‘ cast

•